KNOWING HOW TO LOSE

Chiara Lubich

KNOWING HOW TO LOSE

New City London

First published as *Saper perdere*, 1969
by Città Nuva, Roma
First published in Great Britain 1981
by Mariapolis Ltd.
57 Twyford Avenue, London W3 9PZ
© 1981 New City London

Nihil obstat
Imprimatur

Set, printed and bound in Great Britain by
Fakenham Press Limited, Fakenham, Norfolk

ISBN 0 904287 16 5

Contents

FOREWORD

IS IT POSSIBLE for one person truly to love another? Am I able to love you for you and not for me? And when it comes to God, do I not use him as a prop for my own lack of maturity?

This collection of short reflections will help us to see that true love between persons is possible and that our love of God is the fulfilment of our personal freedom. Again and again the meditations return to the first Christian, Mary, who emerges as the freest human being there has ever been. We discover that she knew how to love because she knew how to lose. Often we want to love, but we are not free to love, because things and emotional values conquer our desire for personal values. Mary conquered her freedom so that she loved persons for their own sake, not for herself.

This is brought out very clearly in 'Knowing How To Lose'. We are introduced to the heart of the woman who is losing the One she loved, and her special relationship with him.

Desolated, she can still stand by his cross,[1] completely one with his own losing of everything.[2] Her love is so strong and so true that she is completely free even of the God-man who is her son, and of being his mother, insofar as these are for herself. Her love is without conditions.

So Mary is the model of the twentieth-century person who wants to love non-exploitively, and who wants a relationship with God which is the fulfilment of his or her human maturity. But especially the Desolated One who emerges in many of those meditations will rekindle love in many who feel they cannot love, or that they are without God. She can show us that in losing all, we have received the All who are Love, so that in God we become free to love every person without any conditions.

FOR ME

SPEAKING OF JESUS, St Paul writes: '. . . and he gave his life for me.'[3] Each of us can repeat those words of the Apostle: *for me*. My Jesus, if you have died for me – *for me* – how can I doubt your mercy? And if I can believe in that mercy with faith which teaches me that a God has died for me, how can I not risk everything to return this love?

For me. Here is the formula which wipes out the solitude of the most lonely; raises into God every poor man, belittled by the whole world; fills every heart to the brim and makes it spill over onto those who either do not know or do not remember the Good News.

For me. For me, Jesus, all those sufferings? For me that cry?

Oh! You will certainly not let my poor soul be lost nor many others, but you will do everything . . . if only because we have cost you too much.

You gave birth to me for Heaven, as my

mother did for earth. You are always thinking of me, only of me, as you do of each and every person.

You give me more courage to live my Christian life than if I had the whole universe at my back to spur me on.

For me. Yes, for me.

And so, Lord, let me also say especially for the years that remain: *for You.*

TODAY A LOT is said about the role of the laity. And perhaps we would see more clearly who the lay person is and how the lay person is also 'Church', if a better and fuller explanation were given of certain aspects of the life of Mary. It seems to us that she is the model of the lay person, even though she is exceptional and unique.

We Catholics do not make a God of Mary, as we are often accused of doing, but, since love and faith have led us to the discovery of all that makes her *special*, we often place her to one side, far away from us. We place her in a sphere which is hers, but it is not the only sphere in which she belongs.

In her we praise the Mother of God, the Immaculate, the Assumed, the Queen, but not the *perfect Christian*, the fiancée, the bride, the mother, the widow, the virgin, the model of every Christian. She, like us lay people, cannot offer Christ sacramentally to the world for,

5

again like us, she is not part of the hierarchy. Yet she is always very active in the Church, sharing in its maternity through the charity which burns in her heart, which is the source of her sacrifice with which she shares in the sacrifice of her son.

Mary, a lay person like us, reminds us that the essence of Christianity is love and that each priest and each bishop too before being a priest or bishop must first of all be a true Christian, living the crucifixion as Jesus did who founded his Church on the Cross.

Furthermore, by highlighting in the Church the fundamental aspect of love that makes it 'One' – in the way that the Trinity is 'one' – Mary presents the Bride of Christ to the world in the way Jesus wanted her to be and in the way that all men today are waiting for: ordered charity, organized charity. And only by emphasizing this, its fundamental aspect, can the Church worthily fulfil today its function of contact and dialogue with the world, which, although often less interested in the hierarchy, is responsive to the witness of love in the Church, the soul of the world.

'CHARITY... THE GREATEST of all ... it does not come to an end.'[4] Here is the reason we all need to be charity, putting it in everything so that we can set out on the track leading to eternity.

To put ourselves immediately into charity is to put ourselves into what remains: God.

God, who must be chosen by us as the all of our life and be chosen again each moment. Holy Scripture puts it so splendidly: 'Love the Lord your God with all your heart, with all your soul, with all your strength. The commands I give you today are to be written on your heart. You shall repeat them to your children and speak of them to them whether at rest in your house or walking abroad at your lying down or at your rising. Fasten them on your hand as a sign and wear them on the forehead as a phylactery. Write them on the doorposts of your house and on your gates.'[5]

WHAT DO YOU WANT US TO ASK YOU?

'WHATEVER YOU PRAY for in faith you will receive.'[6] Well then, Lord, what do you want us to ask you? For the reunion of the separated brethren, as quickly as possible, as so many desire? Did not the Pope say one Sunday that, in spite of the fact that a miracle seemed necessary, 'perhaps the time is near'?

And if you still see the time as far off, could we not bring it closer with the help of Mary, who certainly desires the reunion of her children, and with the accord of the Holy Spirit, who, since he blows towards unity, is overjoyed that this should happen as soon as possible?

And then, and then ... we ask you for the conversion of atheists: yes, because many of them are good and are in good faith, and are fighting with strength and constancy for a cause that seems just to them. And certainly they are not lukewarm, worthy thereby of being 'spat out',[7] but are often capable of becoming ardent christian witnesses.

Again we ask you that your Church, your Spouse, may shine and be radiant in unity according to your desire, as was so often expressed in the recent Council.

IT IS USELESS to deny it! We are not Christians as Jesus would like us to be except in rare cases.

For example, if we observed the Beatitudes we would not often find forced endurance and repressed rebellion in the hearts of the children of God, but gentleness dedicated to a peaceful possession of the earth.

We would not know bitter resignation in places of sorrow, but homes where hymns of thanksgiving rise to the Lord, so far as is possible amidst tears.

We would not find souls engulfed in the mire of the world, but eyes that – although in the world – see persons and events in God.

We would not meet poverty as the mother of spiritual misery, but as the well-spring of the Kingdom of God.

We would not know hatred, vengeance, hardness of heart, because all human relationships would be pervaded by mercy.

Instead the world is an endless sadness; the places of weeping, perennial weeping, and the places where the dead are, are forgotten even though they are alive in the life which lasts.

WHEN WE READ the life of St Peter Eymard, founder of the Blessed Sacrament Fathers, it seems to be a continual discovery of the infinite treasures contained in the Eucharist.

The saint appears immersed in the Eucharist, as if in the heaven of his soul, as if in the cell of his religious life. His is the famous phrase: 'Our century is sick because it does not adore'.[8]

To adore.

At times what a thirst we feel to adore. Adoration means kneeling down, very low, your head on the earth, above all in the spiritual sense, in front of the Creator, the Lord, whom the creature in us calls out for.

To adore is to make oneself nothing before God and to say to him: 'You are everything', that is to say, 'You are what you are', and I possess the immense privilege of life in order to recognize this.

St Peter Eymard discovered certain aspects of the spiritual life which have since become the inheritance of the Church. What Pope Pius XI said about his method of prayer is wonderful. 'Peter Eymard gathered up from every age, from the most intimate sense of tradition ... the thought which sees in Jesus Eucharist that totality of magnificent things where the essence and practice of worship is summarized, and becomes sublime: adoration, thanksgiving, reparation and supplication. Here is the whole of religion, all the attitudes that humanity can and must assume before the Creator.'[9]

IT IS 'HOW' THAT COUNTS

THERE ARE DAYS when, humanly speaking, things go better, and days when they go less well. And once again you repeat the happy experience that, in the present life that you are given, it does not matter whether things go well or less well. What matters is *how* you live, because in that *how* is charity and this alone gives value to everything.

Those who love God keep his word.[10]

During the day we should constantly remember that we will not take joys or sorrows into Paradise. Even giving our bodies to be burnt, if done without charity, is nothing.[11]

It is the same with works of the apostolate. Even knowing the language of angels, without charity, is worthless.[12]

Also works of mercy. Even giving everything to the poor, without charity, is worthless.[13]

We shall take into Paradise *how* we have lived all these things; if it has been according to

14

God's word, which enables us to express our charity.

So let us get up happy each day, rain or shine; and let us remember that what will have value in our day is the amount of God's word we have 'assimilated' during it. In this way, Christ will have lived in us during the day and will have given value to the deeds we accomplish, either by our direct participation or by our prayer and suffering. And, at the end, these works will follow us. [14]

In short we can admire how the word of God, the Truth, makes us free . . . [15] free from circumstances, free from this body of death, [16] free from trials of the spirit, free from the world which closing around us wishes to deform the beauty and fullness of God's Kingdom within us.

AFTER A DAY in which we have sincerely tried to love our neighbour for Jesus, it often happens that we experience feelings which take us towards God or move us deeply. I think we should not attach excessive importance to them, but neither can we despise them. It is certain that, if the Lord feels himself loved, He draws us to himself.

At first we are drawn to him just as we are: a union of the human and the divine.

We observe these feelings are divine because they are God-directed, beautiful, pure, although still a little heavy because they are mingled with the human.

Gradually we respond to grace, loving Him in deeds and remember: 'Not everyone who says Lord, Lord.'[17] And we feel our love, which should not be angelic but human-divine, begin to resemble that of the heart of Jesus, where everything is light and full of purity.

Then it is God who loves in us with greater transparency.

BECAUSE 'GOD IS love'[18] He became flesh: He became a baby in order to grow up and die for us and take us back – lost sheep – to the Father.

Whoever understands charity shares in Christmas, and charity is understood by whoever loves. And, as Augustine says, whoever does not break unity, loves.

This great doctor of the Church helps to distinguish the Christian from the heretic with these words: 'He has the spirit of God who says that Jesus came in the flesh and says it not with words but deeds, not just by speaking but by *loving*. He is not of God's spirit who does not recognize that Jesus came in the flesh; denying it not by words but by his life, not by his mouth but by his actions.

'Now ask a heretic: Did Christ come in the flesh? Yes . . . And yet he denies it . . . He states it in words but denies it in deeds. Christ came in the flesh to die for us and no man has greater love than he who gives his life for his friends.

17

Now you do not have charity because by your pride you divide the unity of the Church.'[19]

If among the separated brethren, inheritors, often innocently, of grave errors, a spirit of ecumenism has been released in these times which is drawing them slowly but surely back towards unity, it means that the whole of christianity is becoming fragrant with a splendid, imminent, new Christmas. It is not only saying with words that Christ came in the flesh, but confirming it by deeds: with charity that wants to recompose unity.

YOU FIND THE ALL

A MINOR ACCIDENT can confront you with possibilities that range from nothing to everything; possibilities which can even make you feel the nearness of death.

Then everything crumbles afresh before you, and you find yourself with the *All* – God, and, in Him, all that the Christian ideal of your life has formed in your life day by day: that splendour of light that calls forth love and fullness of life in every circumstance, even if you are nailed to an operating-table or a death-bed or are in agony.

It is strange. But I have experienced it. At last I have felt that nothingness coincides with everything, and that I lack nothing because I have the All that I want.

And thinking of death, you see and experience that it is only in *living* that you prepare yourself to die well – without any special religious practices or any new attitudes.

When suspicions about death skim near you,

it is suffering that helps to pierce the curtain of cloud still covering the Heaven beyond – while you are still perhaps living in Heaven here on earth.

And if afterwards, someone removes this anxiety and believe they are calming you, they succeed, also because 'the flesh is weak',[20] and you are relieved but the spirit may feel a slight shudder: 'Paradise lost! Now, when at last I was going to see the Trinity!'

Then with a wing-beat of your soul you embark on a longer flight and ask God for sufferings, all the sufferings you need in order 'to do Purgatory' here on earth.

And you feel that God listens and Mary prepares to equip one of her children with the complete dowry they need for the final period of their lives.

CHANGE

ON ASH WEDNESDAY Pope Paul VI gave a talk on penitence. After drawing attention to the reduction the Church had made in physical penances, he explained how 'penitence' means above all *metanoia* or 'change of heart', and he spoke about the interior change, more than exterior, that is brought about by the essence of Christianity: charity.

'Penitence is not a backward step in modern life and teaching. On the contrary, it is a step forward, since it is more inwardly developed, and more demanding in terms of self-examination and the development of one's own personality, in order to make it what it should be: a Christian personality.

'Now since the essence of Christianity is charity, each of us should face the renunciation, sacrifice, self-denial and perseverance that charity demands; even to the point of reaching some form of abdication of ourselves and our ego. We must die inwardly if we want to be born again...'[21]

Then he spoke of prayer, the great penance. He said: 'Then there remains the great penance, that of directing our soul towards God, prayer. *Elevatio mentis ad Deum*. (The raising of the mind to God.) Even this form of spiritual duty we consider to be easy, since it is familiar to us, it fills our days, our timetables. But it is indispensable to pray well...'[22]

To pray well.

This reminds me of the advice given by a loved one who was dying: 'You need to pray well during life, because at the end you have no more time.'

WITH YOUR FEET ON THE GROUND

SOMETIMES 'SOMEONE' URGES us to live constantly in the *supernatural*, that is to say, in *absolute uncertainty* about any human situation whatsoever – plans, journeys, health, future – so that we may *live in the certainty of reality*, which is to live the present moment in a divine way, knowing and willing what God would have us know and will in the present moment. This is why the soul is commanded by Jesus to 'watch' since we know neither the day nor the *hour* of His coming, and we might add, of His every coming.

He continually comes in each moment, in His will, which may seem sad or beautiful to man's eyes, but which in reality is He himself: it is his love.

This spiritual attitude means that in the life of our soul, we have our feet on the ground – in the promised land of the Kingdom of Heaven, which can and must be lived already in this life – and there is no danger of falling. There is no danger of falling into sin, illusions, delusions or anxiety.

A PROTECTOR

OH, ST JOSEPH! Perhaps I have prayed to you too little . . . I ask your pardon.

I have spoken about you, but I have not spoken with you, and yet you have said so much to us by your silence, by your readiness to carry out the wishes of God, by your daily work which teaches all men, especially the poor of the world, to offer up their own labour.

You are the Protector of the Church, and Pope John XXIII gave you a special position in it.

We desire to have a deep devotion towards you, because you protected Mary and Jesus and because you are a model of all the virtues.

St Joseph, we commend to you the unity of the Church; the orders, the religious movements, the families. Take care of the young people and the children so that they are not led astray by the evil of the world, but, guarded also by you, they may walk according to God's plans.

A COMPLETE DIVINE FAMILY

THE SOUL WHO is Christ's bride, the virgin consecrated to God, *is not alone.* She is in reality married to Someone who shows her, especially when her body is weak, all the divine power of an inner strength which is nothing but grace.

In the world we often think that the virgin is alone and this may already seem heroic to those who are well intentioned.

But it is not so. In her heart is the Kingdom of God and her soul is in intimate communion with the Trinity who dwell there.

The virgin is a complete divine family. There is she herself with God in her and, if she is faithful, the souls which are born or are reborn in this marriage, from both partners.

THE TRUE CHRISTIAN

NICHOLAS OF FLÜE was the father of ten children, a peasant farmer, a soldier, a politician, a magistrate. He was united to God and, with his wife Dorothy's agreement, in order to do the will of God, he withdrew to a corner of his farm to be a hermit. Leaving his eldest son as head of the family, he lived contemplating for twenty years, keeping a total fast through a divine miracle.

Although immersed in contemplation, he was 'the father of his country', saving it at a most critical moment of internal strife. He also acted as adviser to politicians of neighbouring countries.

Such a life stuns and amazes you. But what struck me most was his reply to a bishop, who had been sent to question him about his fasting.

'Which is the greatest virtue and the one most pleasing to the Lord?'

'Obedience,'[23] was the reply.

And then, out of obedience, he ate a mouthful of bread and drank a sip of wine with great effort, and the bishop embraced him.

This is the true Christian: he who obeys.

And today, especially today, we need to remember this.

TO MOVE MOUNTAINS

'IF YOU HAVE faith and do not doubt at all . . .
even if you say to this mountain, "Rise up
and throw yourself into the sea", it will be
done.'[24]

How many demands we have made on you,
Lord! How many mountains we have asked
you to move, private mountains unknown to
others, and mountains that others may have
known about.

Remove the mountain of imperfections and
omissions from all of us and bring into our
souls the mountain of graces you wish to dis-
tribute to the world, but which the world
refuses!

Remove the uncertainty which sometimes
envelops our soul, and bring to it the mountain
of strong hope, the theological virtue which
reaches the soul with the fragrance of certainty.

Remove the mountain of veils that covers the
shining face of your Church, and show her to

the world clothed in that beauty that proclaims her to all as your Bride.

Remove the mountain of intellectual pride, and restore to our hearts the mountains of that genuine and honest faith which only the simple and the humble know and possess, and which flows abundantly from the chair of Peter.

Bring mountains of grace to your children who are dying today and do not want to hear any mention of you, so that by your grace they may believe in your love!

Remove from the world the mountain of the fear of war, and give back to the world the mountain of peace (oh, indeed at this hour it is a mountain!) for which all of us implore you.

Remove the mountain which you, Mary, the saints, and the angels would ask to be removed if you were in our place, so that the Kingdom of God may come and His glory blaze forth.

HOPE IS A great virtue.

Why is it that sometimes we are not completely happy? Why are we overshadowed by suffering, tears, and set-backs?

It is because we lack hope. If we stop to think about it and take even a quick general look at the Gospel, we will see that hope is the Gospel style because there we see the faithful expectation of God's promises, which are the treasures of the Gospel.

To renew our Christian life, to give it the transparent smile of gospel children, we now need the virtue of hope, lived with perseverance.

'The God of hope'[25] is what St Paul called the Lord.

Yes, this is precisely the point. May the one true God fill you 'with all joy and peace'.[26] These are the two things which the world lacks and are the gift which the Christian should give to the world.

31

'POPULORUM PROGRESSIO'

'POPULORUM PROGRESSIO' IS marvellous, powerful, totally revolutionary. It expresses an avant-garde Christianity, displaying all the purest riches in innovatory ideas gathered by Pope Paul VI from the Scriptures, the working of God's grace, and the signs of the times.

You need to read it several times to understand what a change the world could expect if it were to put it into practice.

Mankind will be helped to become a single brotherhood. We must do everything the Pope says, even if to some it may seem a utopia. But it will no longer seem so, when the cogs of human structures have been oiled by charity.

For the Holy Father, development is the new name of peace. And when we look at the heart of his encyclical, we see this is synonymous with a world where universal brotherhood is practised. This announces and is the necessary condition for the fulfilment of Jesus' testament: we are all brothers, we all help one another, goods are held in common on a global scale, and there is a world authority 'capable of effective action on a juridical and political level'.[27]

This is God's plan for the world today. Man's task, the task of each of us, is to achieve it.

ANOTHER WORK OF MERCY

IT SEEMS STRANGE but we do not always understand the value of a work of mercy that does not appear to be one: that of *putting up with annoying people*.

In our communal life as Christians, we often do love one another according to Jesus' example since this is his commandment. But sometimes despite everyone's good will, sharply opposed characters meet and live together. Humanly speaking, these characters seem to have so little in common that it is a joy and a comfort to us to know it is a work of mercy to put up with them. Our forbearance over their behaviour, their awkward manner, their continual petulance, the way we lovingly ignore these small things, this is a *work of mercy*; just as much as feeding the hungry and visiting the sick. Our putting up with annoying people is one of the works that will be asked of us at our final examination.

WHAT HEROIC VIRTUES shone in Mary as she stood, '*stabat*',[28] at the foot of the cross on Calvary.

What a mother! To have a son who is God himself, and to see him die in that way . . .

And she didn't give up! Only her being the '*Mother of God*' could have enabled her to do so much. How else can we explain it? And there, we were born, made children of God by Jesus and children of Mary by Jesus handing us over to her.

There the Virgin is explicitly the Mother of the Church. But what a price she had to pay for the Bride of Christ! Christ himself. From this we can deduce how the Church truly is the Body of Christ.

Mary, in your love for us, give us a little of your faith, of your hope, of your charity, of your strength, of your perseverance, of your constancy, of your humility, of your purity, of your meekness, of your mercy, of all your

35

virtues, which, as we review them, make us understand once more the degree to which you lived them.

It was to you that Jesus entrusted the Church, but because of the passion we have burning in our heart for it, we dare to make our request to you. May the unity of all Christians come quickly.

You are all powerful through grace.

You can do this.

livingCity
P.O. Box 837
Bronx, NY 10465-0837

Name
Address

City ——— St —— Zip

Living City Subscription Form

☐ Sign me up for a subscription to **livingCity**

☐ Bill me   ☐ Payment enclosed

☐ New   ☐ Renewal

Name _____

Address _____

City _____ State ___ Zip ___

Phone (___) _____

☐ Start a subscription for my friends!

Please sign gift card:

_____

Name _____

Address _____

City _____ State ___ Zip ___

(Payment must accompany gifts.)

· One year (11 issues): USA: US$25.00; Canada: US$25.00; Europe and South America: US$50.00; Australia, Africa and Middle East: US$60.00.

· Two years (22 issues): USA: US$45.00.

Please make checks payable to Living City

IN THE TWELFTH century St Bernard said in a famous sermon, 'Today all my high philosophy consists in knowing that Jesus is and that he was crucified.'[29]

And when Bernard set out with his first companions to follow the road God had shown him, choosing God alone through the way of the cross, 'his life with the brethren', as William of St Thierry says, 'was charity . . .[30] and those who saw how they loved one another, recognized that God was in them'.[31]

A stream of people hurried to see . . . whom? God, who in some way was manifesting himself through the mutual love of the monks.

This is the eternal witness which the world today is also waiting for, perhaps more than at any other time. And God provides this witness. For despite what the usual critics of religion say, there is a spring time about to explode in the heart of the Church; in the midst of the Catholic world that is lukewarm and vacillating, in the midst of the Christian world that is still divided, in the world of Islam, and even in the world which is mainly atheistic.

And this time the flowering of charity is not among monks, but among people from all walks of life, both young and old, and of every nationality. They love one another as Christ taught and flocks of people attracted by God – who lives among these authentic Christians – are again a phenomenon in the twentieth century.

NOURISHING OURSELVES WITH THE WORD

SPEAKING OF THE word of God, Pope Paul VI has said '... His word is one of the ways in which He is present among us...'

'How does Jesus make himself present in souls? Through a vehicle, namely the communication of the word; something so normal in human relationships, but which here becomes sublime and mysterious: the divine thought is communicated, the Word is communicated, the Son of God made Man...'[32]

On various occasions, such as a spiritual worry or a suffering, I have fed on the word of God and my soul has felt fulfilled.

And then I realized that this communion with Jesus, in his word, is possible in each second of my life, and therefore I can feed on Him in each moment.

This experience gave me an immense joy, for the Gospel is not a book of consolations where we only take refuge for answers in moments of suffering, but it is a code containing all the laws of life, for every circumstance of life. These laws are not just to be read, but are to be 'eaten' with our soul, and they then make us like Christ in each instant.

Then every aspect of the day, whether joyful, sorrowful, ordinary, extraordinary, becomes only minimally important or even of no importance whatsoever. When compared to one another, they are indistinguishable, because we see that the only important thing is Christ who with his words fills them and lives them.

—

THE VIRTUE THAT DOES NOT DISAPPOINT

'HOPE DOES NOT disappoint.'[33]

This phrase from Scripture is so beautiful. St Paul says that patience comes from suffering, and experience from patience, and from experience there comes the hope[34] of good things in the next life . . . and also in this life.

This is so very logical. But it is the logic of the supernatural life. Yes, it is so. In the daily trials of life, by exercising patience in charity, we receive inner illumination, this is the experience. And this experience which knows and penetrates to the heart of everything, teaches us exactly how to move forward without losing heart, without self-deception, without becoming depressed or elated. It teaches us how to make good progress. And from this comes the hope of reaching the good things promised in the next life, and the hundred-fold promised in this life.

This lesson taught us by experience, which inclines the soul towards hope, is like a light lit under a tapestry, woven from the trials of the day. Light shines through the tapestry and burst forth above it. We realize that hope, having flowered from the experience of supernatural life within us, is one of the highest virtues and is very close to charity.

In fact, St Paul says: '. . . hope does not disappoint us, because God's love has been poured into our hearts through the Holy Spirit who has been given to us.'[35]

'EUREKA'

MARY DESOLATE IS *the* saint.

I want to re-live her in her mortification.

I want to know how to be alone with God like her, in the sense that, even while with my brothers, I feel inspired to make my whole life an intimate dialogue between the soul and God.

I must mortify all the words, thoughts, and deeds which are outside the moment of God, in order to set them like jewels in the moment reserved for them.

Mary Desolate gives us the certainty of holiness. She is the perennial source of union with God, a vase overflowing with joy.

Mary Desolate.

This is my *'eureka'*. Yes, I have found it. I have found the way.

IF IT WERE THE TIME FOR HOSANNAS

I HAVE READ of St Margaret of Cortona:
'Brother Giunta (her spiritual director) writes
that one night, when Satan had the evil inspi-
ration of obsessing the saint with her fame, she
went up the stairs to the balcony of her house
and, weeping, began shouting out: "Wake up
people of Cortona! Wake up! I'm telling you to
wake up and stone me and drive me far away,
as soon as you can. I'm the sinner who
committed this sin and this sin against God
and my neighbour . . ." And she proceeded to
list, at the top of her voice, all the faults of her
life.'[36]

It is a marvellous lesson in humility and one
that tells us the truth about ourselves.

If we are called to take part in the adventure
of doing God's work in the Church, and if the
time of approval, of triumph, of 'hosannas',
has come, let us be careful to distinguish the
work of God from ourselves. We must distinguish between His grace and ourselves,

between what He achieves through us and what we are.

The devil may want to use our arrogance and pride by making us thieves who steal for ourselves what belongs to God.

Let us repeat with Augustine, 'Lord, may I know myself and know you.' Yes, because true humility does not consist in saying you do nothing or denying all the good we have achieved, but in giving God his right place and putting ourselves in ours.

TO LOVE THE cross. This is the only thing we must remember. To love the cross means controlling our faculties so that they go along the track of the divine will. And if they refuse, tame them. And if they are going astray, prevent them. And if they want to escape, constrain them and snatch them back with violence.

If we do not love the cross, true love for God and our brothers does not exist in our hearts.

THE CHRISTIAN DIMENSION

'I SENT YOU to reap a harvest you had not worked for. Others worked for it and you have come into the rewards of their labour.'[37]

Jesus sees the whole of mankind before him. The prophets – those who sowed in the past – are just as much present to him as the apostles, whom He so ardently desires to send out to reap.

So the joy – heaven – will be for everyone.

We must always have this vision of life: the living and the dead always equally present in a dimension of truly Christian charity.

What strength and what courage comes from always being, living, and working in the presence of our saints of East and West.

We must make them live again in our souls, so that they may keep on the watch and help each and every one of us to carry out the work that He has entrusted to us.

IT'S AN ILLUSION

THERE'S NO QUESTION about it. We can love the world, because everything in the world is made by God, directly or indirectly. But if it's true that eternity exists, and that Heaven exists, then this life which is so short must be viewed in its proper perspective and given its true meaning.

We are here on trial.

We are here for a purpose and a destiny which do not belong to this moment but to a later moment, in another world.

Our life, which daily becomes more rooted to this earth and the things of this earth, our life which is only concerned with making itself comfortable in this world, is wrong and a total illusion. Indeed, maybe it is worse than an illusion, because one day we will lose it. It will end. And if we act in the way we have just described, then we will lose the next life also. There will be no next life for us!

Yes, we can be men of our times. We can

satisfy modern tastes. But if we want to avoid making a serious mistake, let's first be *eternal* men, who do not die and who follow in the footsteps of those who were truly wise – the saints!

Their life, their austerity, the flight – at least spiritually – from the world, their mortifications, may disturb us, but they are reasonable and sound. The rest is madness, 'Whoever loves his life will lose it, and whoever hates his life in this world will save it.'[39]

TO BE ALIVE AND THINK WE ARE HALF-DEAD

JESUS REVEALS HIMSELF to the Samaritan woman as the Messiah and announces the gift He brings: grace. With grace the soul is satisfied: God is in it and fills it.

Indeed, the water Jesus puts in the soul becomes 'a spring of water welling up'. It does not stand still. It does not remain the same. It is alive and offers life ... 'even to eternal life'.[39]

Eternity, therefore, begins here on earth. It is up to us to put ourselves in this circuit of light. It is up to us to enjoy the fullness that fills us.

How often – for some people almost always – we live as if we were poor. From this comes sadness and weariness and a clouded outlook on life. And all the time we carry within us a treasure that, if we only knew it, could make us overflow with joy, fill us completely, satisfy our hunger and thirst.

How absurd our Christian life is! To be rich

and believe ourselves poor. To be alive and think we are half-dead. To be always able to give the world a smile and instead show sadness around us.

But when will we convert ourselves? When will the world see the life of Christians manifested like a city on a hill, like a lamp on a stand?

Looking at people from the most varied and distant cities of the world, we often see very little difference between those who have this 'water' and those who do not yet possess it. And we want to bring this water to those who do not have it, to those who unconsciously long for it – even though they do not know it – and leave to languish those who, indifferent and sated with the things of the world, have not the slightest desire to live God's life.

But perhaps the Father will accomplish this revolution. Does not the Gospel say that 'from those who have not it will be taken away and given to those who have already'?[40]

Who knows, perhaps future centuries will witness an emigration of Christianity to countries now pagan, and perhaps it will be these countries who give back to our existing

Christian world, the example of a freshness of divine life that renews everything, just as the birth of a child gives the father and mother who are already mature, the sense of a second youth.

FINDING THINGS AGAIN IN THEIR EXACT PROPORTIONS

THOUSANDS OF FEELINGS, thousands of spiritual affections, thousands of thoughts sometimes fill my mind which is so deeply involved in different activities for the service of the Church: conversations, work, journeys . . .

They are so varied that I carry them with me like a treasure to reflect upon, to analyse; a treasure which often brings great consolation to my heart. And yet all this is a beautiful world which obscures my soul, a wealth which, in a certain way, occupies a space in me where God should be.

I have understood yet again that I must live the present and throw into the Heart of Jesus everything – including holy things – which involved me in the moment that has passed. I must throw them into the heart of Jesus, so that He may look after them, allowing them to grow and develop, and then make me find them again in this new state of maturity, as has so often happened in the past.

This means losing. Knowing how to lose is the law of the Gospel just as Mary Desolate lost even Jesus – her Work – in order to do the will of God, for the sake of God.

'To lose' in order to be completely involved in what God wants for me in the present moment.

To lose everything ... so that God's 'sun' may return into that emptiness, and my thoughts and affections may find in Him their right place and exact proportions, in each holy, important detail. And today, in Him, we find love for the Church Militant, love for the Church Triumphant in its rejoicing, love for the Church in Purgatory in its suffering. And love for tomorrow's Church, which He already sees and loves: the Bride of the Word.

HE WEPT

'JESUS WEPT....'[41]

These words are in the Gospel.

Jesus! Your weeping! Oh! how your weeping consoles us! In it we find our own. Your tears guarantee that you have pity on us, and our weeping, because you yourself experienced this.

Wherever you see tears, you see yourself.

You, who are Beatitude, who are Eternal, Unchangeable, Unmovable, experienced distress in your human soul.

Thank you, Jesus, for your Passion and Death, but thank you also for these brief episodes which make us feel you very close to us, in every hesitation and agitation of our soul.

When we are like this, we remember you and you see yourself again in us; you live again in us and continue your passion in us, your members, for the salvation of those who do not know you.

THE PASSION FOR THE CHURCH

THE PASSION FOR the Church which Pope Paul VI[42] spoke about rules the hearts of true Christians. However, this passion must pass from the level of feeling to the practical level, where love for the whole Church, just as it stands – with its institutions which are the fruit of numerous charisms which the Holy Spirit has poured out and pours out on the Church – calls for knowledge and knowledge calls for new love.

What Christianity teaches in the field of relationships between individuals: love, get to know each other, make yourself one with others to the point of being able to communicate the eventual gifts which God has given you; this approach must be transferred to the social level, and this means getting to know, esteem and love the other movements and works of the Church, creating or developing the reciprocal communion of spiritual goods among them all.

The outcome would be collaboration, willed by the heart and the will, and in this way we would truly serve the Church which we love.

If we were not to do this then our 'passion' for the Church would be purely rhetorical and we would find ourselves in conditions which would shut us off and isolate us.

In addition our love for the Pope would be reduced to ephemeral enthusiasm and sentimentality, because we would not be sharing what he loves with him: the life of the whole of God's Church.

THE ONE AND ONLY GREAT LOVE

TO LOVE GOD with all your strength and, in Him, to love all creatures in an ordered way – this is Christianity.

But perhaps we sometimes go astray because we pass on to the second part too quickly, and interpret it wrongly.

No, what we must do is *love God*, giving to Him our whole being; our time, our work, our love, our intellect.

And to express this, it is also our duty to turn our attention and care and love to those He has created.

But we must do this for Him, in order to *continue* to love Him.

We should be perennial contemplatives. And how we fail! What freedom we would find, however, in this one and only great love. Just the thought of it makes us feel freed from the countless bonds which social life ties round us.

PRAYER AND PENANCE?

THE WONDERFUL MOMENT is past when the Pope visited Fatima on 13th May, 1967, and the pilgrims there had the joy of often seeing him, accompanied by Lucia. For the simple, honest faith of many, this, I think, must have been almost a heavenly vision, a miraculous vision.

But what do the words mean that were repeated by the Madonna to the children: 'prayer' and 'penance'?

Prayer means giving devotions and prayers their place by putting them before everything else, both as a whole and in terms of their content, in the knowledge that when this has been done, everything has been done.

And *penance* – as St Lawrence Giustiniani also says – means seeking the daily cross and loving it.[43]

This is what we try to do.

What comfort and encouragement this fact gives us.

Yes, if we are true Christians, we too will be souls pleasing to God, evangelical souls who fulfil the requests made by Mary when she appeared in the world to ask for its conversion.

IF OUR ONE object in life was to be perfect towards God and towards each of our brothers, we would have accomplished everything.

Yes, because being perfect in charity towards God means being perfect in the observance of each of his laws. It means living perfectly that charity which the Holy Spirit has poured into our hearts and which makes us 'small suns' beside the Sun.

Knowing that 'God is love'[44] and that we are his children, his plan for us could be the fulfilment of Jesus' saying, *'Dii estis'* – 'You are gods':[45] love beside Love, little Jesus' next to Jesus, little Marys next to Mary.

Perfect in charity means having a perfect love towards our brothers, which develops in us all the Christian virtues, giving us the truly highest poverty, transparent purity, total humility, perseverance right to the end without our realizing it, patience which is not a burden . . .

Perfect in charity not only towards whoever passes next to us, but towards everyone means seeing what is beautiful in all the vocations of the Church and seeing each one's characteristic beauty: it means seeking what is positive in all peoples, and with this committed attitude, contributing to universal brotherhood and peace.

It means valuing the Christianity that is truly alive within the separated Churches or communities; it means understanding the good aspirations of all men even those far away from Christ, and therefore it means taking the first step in order to offer them the full truth.

To be perfect in charity means having your heart and mouth at the disposal of the Holy Spirit, who, through us can heal wounds both near at hand and far away, bringing consolation to many and winning souls.

'FATHER, I WANT those you have given me to be with me where I am, so that they may always see the glory you have given me because you loved me before the foundation of the world. Father, Righteous One, the world has not known you but I have known you, and these have known that you have sent me. I have made your name known to them and will continue to make it known, so that the love with which you loved me may be in them, and so that I may be in them.'[46]

He wants to give us Paradise.

Where He will be, He wants us to be also; He wants to enable us to see His eternal glory.

And invoking the Father reminding him that He is 'righteous', He invokes for us – as distinct from the world which has not known Him – the very love with which the Father has loved Him.

What fathomless depth; Jesus in his testament reveals himself as God more than ever.

There appears to be nothing of man in these

words that are so completely Trinitarian, yet, at the same time we feel the heart of a friend, of a brother, of a loving teacher, of a father who gives to his own *everything* that he can: participation in his divinity.

I DO NOT WANT TO BE RESIGNED

WITH GOD'S GRACE I am not content with merely being resigned one day – the day of my agony and death.

No, in the eyes of others, who are still enjoying life here on earth, anyone who has reached this stage belongs to a category – the sick, the dying – and a special atmosphere is created around them, albeit a supernatural one.

But why don't we always live *as* if today were our last day and our last hour?

Before dying Christ said: 'Father, glorify your Son.'[47] It was a beginning, not an ending. And St Peter speaks of 'the crown of glory'.[48]

This is Christianity.

So I shall accept all the daily sufferings as 'rehearsals' for the trial, which is the agony and final struggle. I shall accept them as training exercises to develop patience, perseverance, trust in God, and a passion for the cross which will carry me to glory.

TWO GREAT LOVES

IN ORDER TO be like Mary we must model our spirit and our body on Christ Crucified and in particular on his spiritual sufferings, avoiding any excessive analysis that leads to the purely 'human'. For if we embrace these spiritual sufferings, desiring and willing them as best we can, we are taken into the 'divine'.

Without the cross, a Christian is not a Christian. Grignon de Montfort says the cross will proceed us into Heaven and through it we will have glory; through it we are 'legitimate members of Christ'. [49]

The cross is the root of charity. We cannot be children of God if we are not like the Son of God, who through the cross is the Saviour.

With the cross our life is solid; it is well planted and protected against storms; it is a life which is not exposed to variations. With the cross we go ahead confidently.

The cross will make us wise among men, even if they consider us fools.

It will purify us and fit us to bring God's Kingdom to souls, which is something we have to pay for, just as we have to pay for being 'generators' of Christ in our midst.

Two great loves must possess our heart: Mary as the point of arrival and the cross as the means of being another Mary in the world and so fulfilling God's plans.

God wants us to be little saviours, who look the evils of the world in the face and remedy them. He wants us to be little saviours who know that they have *not* come for the healthy but for sinners and those farthest away from Him.

WHAT A DESTINY!

ST JOHN SAYS: 'But to all who received him, who believed in his name, he gave power to become children of God: born not of blood . . .'[50]

Perhaps we do not think enough about our destiny as Christians.

Perhaps we do not witness enough to the infinite abyss that exists between a son of God and a son of the flesh, born of the will of man.

Perhaps we do not understand how much has happened to us through meeting in our life the Word who became flesh, in whom we have believed. It is this belief in Him which makes us sons of God.

This is the source of our gratitude to God for having chosen us and of our responsibility to communicate to others the message of salvation.

THE LAMB OF God: this is how John the Baptist defines Jesus. He immediately sees him as a victim which God – rather than men – has chosen for himself.

The same should apply to each Christian, indeed must apply to each Christian.

We are born to be sacrificed like Christ and then to share with him in his glory.

We must await that day and that moment like a bride awaits her bridegroom. That hour comes for everyone and, what is more, it comes like a thief, when we are not expecting it.

It is life well lived, moment by moment, in readiness for that hour, which has true meaning.

Yes, here below we should create the foundations of a better world for our brothers who are yet to come because we already love them as Christ has taught us. (And the more we spread Christianity the more we will do this.) But we, for our own sake, should stay alert, continually awaiting the call to enter into life, into a Kingdom which is not of this world.

My God, what a mystery is the life you have given us, and what a trial – death – it has to undergo to reach its goal, its home.

Thank you for coming on earth and showing us the Way, for making Yourself the Way. We, lost in you, will always be in the light, even though we are immersed in the deepest darkness.

Thank you for being born, for living and for 'dying for us',[51] for me.

For dying: Yes, for dying. If You had not died, how would we have been able to face death? Instead, even in that supreme act, we will think of You and die with You.

We should make Jesus who dies an ideal. For many this could be the source of an unexpected flow of life.

A POWERLESS 'STABAT'

LOVING MARY DESOLATE means many
things: not only does it mean 'losing', knowing
how to lose all we have and are in the Heart of
Jesus in order to find it again at the opportune
moment, multiplied and developed; but it
often means staying like Mary at the foot of a
living crucifix, and not succeeding or being
able to take away from that soul and that suffering flesh the affliction which torments it almost
to the point of despair.

We would prefer to be in the person's place
ourselves. But instead our part is to be present
without doing anything – in front of the grain
of corn which, by dying, is germinating – certain of resurrection and of the fruits to come.
For the present we stand there in a suffering
'stabat', which is not a comfort to the person we
love, but which like incense rises parallel with
them towards heaven, imploring mercy for us
who, together, consume our life.

It is the powerless 'stabat'.

Mary, you who know us, you who know certain sufferings, relieve those who suffer, shorten their time, bring closer the hour of relief.

LIFE IS HARD

JESUS ISSUES THIS invitation: 'Come to me all you who are weary and oppressed, and I will restore you.'[52]

How comforting these words are!

And how inhuman and proud are those men who don't want to consider the Gospel and also the other sacred books as books of consolation.

But let us openly admit that there is suffering here on earth and that life is hard!

And what does this suffering call for if not someone who consoles?

Yes, life is hard and God who is love knows this, and has always taken this into consideration: first through the Messiah awaited from the world's beginning then through the Messiah who came.

Thus, for whoever believes, everything has an answer.

And the balance is restored.

AN EXCEPTIONAL SAINT

'THE BRIDE IS only for the bridegroom; and yet the bridegroom's friend, who stands there and listens, is glad when he hears the bridegroom's voice. This same joy I feel, and now it is complete. He must increase, I must decrease.'[53]

This finale of St John the Baptist in John's Gospel is marvellous! It is in itself the programme for Christian life. In experiencing these words and their weight, we certainly understand just how exceptional this saint was.

They are such important words that they demonstrate how extraordinary is this soul who spoke them. In fact, John the Baptist is pre-sanctified.

John, who symbolizes Baptism because he gives it – even though only with water – and announces it, was treated in a unique way by God in regard to this sacrament. And how beautiful God is in his saints!

And here, in my view, we cannot continue reading the Gospel unless we first put into practice for a little while those words of life: 'He must increase, I must decrease.'

How? By knowing how to lose. By knowing how to lose in the present moment everything which is not the will of God.

THERE IS ANOTHER WORLD

'HE WHO COMES from above is above all others; he who is born of the earth is earthly himself and speaks in an earthly way.'[54]

This is the difference between Jesus and ourselves. He comes from on high. 'You come down from the stars...' runs the popular Italian Christmas carol.

Jesus brings Heaven to us on earth. He speaks about what He has seen and heard.

There is another world besides the one that meets our eyes: the world from which Jesus comes down. And there you see and hear.

We come from the earth.

Here lies the difference between what we say and what 'He who comes from Heaven' says. His are *eternal words*.

The life of the person who keeps the Gospel in his heart during every day of his existence is the only life spent intelligently.

And such a person finds his supreme ideal in incarnating the Words of Heaven.

WITHOUT EXCLUDING ANYONE

'IF YOU ONLY knew what God is offering and who it is that is saying to you: "Give me a drink. . . ."'[55]

Jesus does not stop to answer the Samaritan woman about the quarrels existing between Jews and Samaritans. His is a language which strikes, enraptures, transports from earth to heaven.

His heart seems to burst from his chest in its desire to give the best thing he has brought to earth: the gift of God. He wants to give two things to men: grace and the knowledge of He who gives this 'living water'.

'Living water!'[56]

It's magnificent! Do we realize this? A living water. Living. Life lives in whoever knows and possesses life. It is the same with God's grace: it is the soul's life.

Jesus is amazing! How little we know him unless we read the Gospel with love.

In fact, we have often made our own image

of him, following some worn-out traditional form of piety. But in the Gospel he appears as he is: He is God. He continually reveals himself to be *God*. A God . . . who speaks, who is tired, who walks, who has disciples . . . a Man-God. That's how it is!

And then further on comes that answer.
'I who am speaking to you, I am he'[57]

This reduces us to silence. Yes, Jesus did not exclude anyone. Each man, whoever he is, is deeply worthy of our respect and trust. To the Samaritan woman who has many husbands and not one that is her own, Jesus reveals himself fully. He speaks to her so divinely well, with the simplicity that God alone knows how to use: 'I who am speaking to you, I am he.' I in flesh and bones. Not a ghost. Not someone far away. I, here.

Oh Jesus, I would have liked to have seen you. Your eyes, your face, your manner, your graciousness.

But all we can do is wait a few years, and therefore conclude matters quickly in order to obtain a passport direct to heaven, by paying in advance for purgatory while on earth.

Paradise, Paradise! My God, let this always be my spontaneous desire. When this happens, a great goal will indeed have been reached.

THE SPLENDOUR OF A DISCOVERY

IF I FALTER ever so often, if I sometimes feel I am not anchored to something steady while following the path of my existence and if I live carried along by circumstances a life lived in His service, but without the certainty of belonging totally to God, then this causes me suffering.

I am like someone who is unsure in a rough sea.

I look for You, my God. I look for a means which will give me You, fully and securely. I look for something which fills everything and allows nothing of myself to live.

It is that 'me' which is annoying, as though I bore an illness in my body which I don't know how to free myself from. Then, in these circumstances, I remember the splendour of a discovery; a discovery which gave me the certainty of being able to live for holiness: Mary Desolate, as the mould of perfection in which to place myself.

Therefore, I must choose, more than ever before, this ideal of life, to carry on Mary's work with austerity and with drive. In this way the straining rope will not give way and I will arrive safely in harbour.

YOU SANCTIFY

O HOLY SPIRIT, how grateful we should be to you and yet how little we show it!

We are consoled by the fact that you are completely one with Jesus and with the Father to whom we turn more often than to you, but this does not justify us.

We want to stay with you . . . 'Best consoler, sweet guest of the soul, sweet refreshment.' You are Light, Joy, Beauty.

You attract souls, you inflame hearts and inspire thoughts of holiness that are deep and decisive with unforeseen individual commitments. You achieve what a multitude of sermons could not teach. You sanctify.

Above all, Holy Spirit, take account of our roughness and lack of subtlety and make us devoted to you: you who are so discreet, and yet impetuous and overwhelming, blowing like a timid breeze which few know how to listen to or how to feel. May no day pass without our invoking you, thanking you, adoring you, loving you, without our living as your dedicated disciples.

We ask you for this grace. And cover us in your great light of love, above all in the hour of deepest darkness, when the vision of this life will end in order to dissolve itself into the vision of eternal life.

WHO SAW MOST?

THE RESURRECTION!

John and Peter go to the empty tomb and find the linen cloths on the ground, the shroud on one side.

Mary Magdalene remains there weeping and sees two angels, one where Jesus' head had been and one where his feet had been. She talks to them and then, turning, she sees Jesus.

The apostles didn't see him, and among them was the one Jesus, covered in a special way on account of his innocence as well as for other reasons. 'Blessed are the pure in heart, for they shall see God.'[58] Mary, the sinner, saw the angels and Jesus.

Who saw most on this occasion? Mary Magdalene.

The tears which flowed continually from her eyes, and her vigil outside the tomb, were the signs of a love which believes everything and wants everything. Then later her conversation with the angels and with the person she thought was the gardener, almost as though Jesus were a person in whom she alone was interested. These two things had purified her heart perhaps more than the hearts of the others, to such a degree that she merited seeing heavenly beings and the risen Jesus.

This is the meaning of the Resurrection. Redemption is completed. Death is conquered. Sin is overthrown by mercy poured out in superabundance from the tree of the Cross.

TWO HEARTS

POPE JOHN XXIII combined two devotions in one: the Heart of Jesus in the Blessed Sacrament;[59] and it is certain that this was where he found the nourishment which made him the good Pope, with a heart as big as the whole world, a heart with which all mankind could identify.

We must imitate him, because our heart too must expand to the size of Jesus' heart. And we must also have a living devotion to the heart of Mary, another heart of flesh which is still beating, beating for each of us.

In these two Hearts we will find a true school of formation, the kiln which will make us into true *images* of Christ and of Mary.

NOSTALGIA FOR PARADISE

AT TIMES WE are filled with nostalgia for
Paradise. At times we feel the weight of life
here below and of the wait to be endured.

But straightaway someone calls us from
within to recollect ourselves and be alone with
the Eternal One.

Someone calls us to be consoled and to be
resigned to continuing life like this for as long
as He wants.

In these moments you feel like a child who is
picked up and hugged in its mother's arms.
Nothing is now missing. And while being
refreshed you recover strength and feel that
'No, no', it is not good to go straight to the
eternal enjoyment of what God's goodness has
prepared for us, and besides that would not be
justice, because eternal happiness must be
merited.

So you make decisions to live the Christian
life well, true resolutions of daily heroism, in
order to reach perfection during all the days

that are left of your life. It is as though flowers had sprung up again in the spring sun. And you look and look again in your soul for the best thoughts which in the past gave power to your wings and taking one just as it comes to you at random, you stamp it on your heart as the seal and motto, as the ideal to be lived – at least during that day.

'YOU ARE THE light of the world ... it gives light to all in the house.'[60]

Light 'of the world' ... to 'all in the house'. This is Christianity: a phenomenon which is so strong that the whole world is illuminated by it. 'All in the house.' All, means *all!*

'You are the salt of the earth.'[61]

Our Christianity does not remain inactive in us if we live it as Christ desires; it rushes to 'flavour' the earth, it develops without our realizing it.

These words of Jesus are splendid. They really express what He brought and what He left us.

Besides if the world is now so much more affected by the light of the Gospel than in past centuries, who should this be attributed to?

We cannot imagine how much Christianity is contained in the laws of the world, in the customs of the world, in the whole world.

And all this belongs to Christ. If, for

example, countries which are still Moslem have abolished polygamy, this is not simply due to the Western mentality of an individual in authority. No, it is all due to Christianity which once it sets out penetrates farther than we can imagine.

This is a great encouragement for us.

It brings closer the aim: 'May they all be one.'[62]

It shows us how inspired the Pope is when he promotes dialogue. There is a common foundation to most of mankind, it is the flavour given to the whole earth by the Christian salt.

IF YOUR BROTHER HAS SOMETHING AGAINST YOU

'SO IF YOU are offering your gift at the altar, and there remember that your brother has something against you, leave your gift there before the altar and go; first be reconciled to your brother and then come and offer your gift.'[63]

Divine worship and love among brothers, the love which creates and rebuilds unity, are absolutely inseparable. If a community does not 'fulfil' itself in Christ in full communion it is unfitted, according to the gospel, to offer true worship to God.

In recent years the Second Vatican Council has reawakened this sense of the united community, and the Holy Spirit, blowing in various ways, has removed the dust from the Gospel of charity.

And how we Christians needed this!

That is why we often felt we did not understand the full value of the liturgy. For the most part we are the heirs of an individual religiosity, which is not too concerned about reciprocal charity in the community.

Although the soul retains a certain sense of the mystery surrounding the great liturgical actions, some of them, which have been reduced at times to form without substance, cause incomprehension and a sense of emptiness.

All this because Christianity is often deprived of its true strength: charity. On the other hand, what riches of liturgical experience we can expect from a truly united people of God! The face of the Church would shine beautifully in all its splendour and would attract the world in the same way that Jesus once attracted the crowds.

MANY . . . ONE BODY

THE APOSTLE PAUL goes out, preaches, makes disciples and is almost always chased away, so we could say that persecutions are the cause of the Gospel spreading.

The same must apply to every work of God.

Wherever Paul goes, he sows widely, always leaving a small group of disciples, whom he then encourages by further visits, letters and exhortations. He also spends long periods with them, and creates the church hierarchy amongst them, which continues his work.

And always when Paul returns to communities which have already been established, he brings his disciples up-to-date with the news of all that the Lord has done elsewhere by means of him. And everyone gives glory to God for this.

Here we see how in authentic Christianity, if it is lived well, information and communications among brothers are as essential as the apostolate and everything else. True Christians live the truth 'many . . . one body'. [64]

ONE THING THE world will never understand is the spiritual fruitfulness of virgins married to God.

Just as God chose a virgin to give Christ to the world, in the same way he chooses virgins as channels to prepare the ground for the coming of Christ into souls.

The true virgin is a mother of souls and this is very much more precious in God's eyes than natural motherhood.

But since it is love for God which 'virginizes', whatever state of life we find ourselves in – a mother, a father, a boy, an old man, a fiancé – if they love God and put him first in their scale of values, allowing the Holy Spirit to shape charity in them – they can become mothers and fathers of souls. This gives great possibilities for the growth of the Kingdom of God in the world.

IT IS EASY for the believer to reach the point of offering himself to God. And perhaps there are many who reach this stage.

But many retreat when God accepts the offer and begins to carry out the sacrifice, through the sufferings which cannot be left out unless we wish to remain spiritually sterile.

When this happens God cannot make Himself one with us and we cannot make ourselves one with Him. Our sanctification is compromised, and with it the sanctification of many.

The Mass which we too must celebrate with our life cannot stop at the offertory. It involves being lifted up on the cross and consummation. In fact, in holy communion, it is our soul which enters into God and God who enters into us. And holiness only reigns where God reigns.

TRUST! IF THERE is 'a curse on the man who puts his trust in man',[65] blessed is the man who trusts in God.

We must grow in trust. This means mortifying useless internal dialogues with ourselves and opening up an ever deeper, more intimate dialogue with God, to whom we entrust what we are and what we have.

We need to increase our trust day by day. Besides what could be more intelligent than trusting in God?

But the gift of freedom which God has given us leaves us the alternative of believing or not believing in the Love which is God.

An absurd alternative for someone who has faith. Because if God is and if his being is Love, complete trust in Him is simply the logical consequence.

WHY HAVE MEN with no knowledge, even religious knowledge, become saints solely with the book of the Crucified Christ? Because they have not merely contemplated Him, or venerated Him, kissing His wounds, but have *relived* Him in themselves.

Whoever suffers and is in darkness sees further than the person who is not suffering, just as the sun has to set before we see the stars.

Suffering teaches what can not be learnt in any other way. Suffering holds the highest chair, and is the master of wisdom and whoever has wisdom is blessed.[66] 'Blessed are those who suffer for they shall be comforted'[67] – not only with the reward in the next life, but also with the contemplation of heavenly things in this life.

We should approach those who suffer with the same reverence – indeed with even more reverence, with which we once approached the old, when we expected to be given wisdom by them.

A HEART OF FLESH

WHAT WILL JESUS be like in Paradise? Well, he is certainly glorified as man also.

And Mary Most Holy, his Mother assumed into heaven, is sufficient reward for his life, death and passion through which he preserved her from sin.

Yet his involvement with mankind makes him want us, who are now his brothers, to ascend to the place he has prepared for us.

The desire of a Man-God cannot be understood! But that Heart of flesh which though transfigured, still beats in Heaven, must surely express itself with inexpressible ardour, sublime tenderness, inflamed hope, inexhaustible, most living and active charity.

That Heart, is often venerated with an infantile piety by us, the poor and blind faithful of the true religion, which is so full of light; a piety which the world with its boundless discoveries and all embracing aspirations, no longer understands. That heart is the sun that shines on the whole world, on the whole of mankind.

We must believe in this Heart. We must trust in it. It is a Heart which will never delude anyone. The Heart of Jesus is the greatest hope for every human being; it is the lamp that shines amidst the shadows of every life.

HEART FOR HEART

AT HOLY COMMUNION I thought about the Heart of Jesus; his Heart, which I adore in the eucharist when he comes, or in Paradise where he is eternally, with the Heart of Mary next to him.

I am happy to have understood better the existence, the reality and the immense fortune of having a Heart – and such a Heart – that loves us.

And I considered what my behaviour should be towards the Heart of Jesus.

I had an intuition: *Heart calls for heart.*

'Heart for heart', therefore is the password for my life today and for always; for as long as God wills.

Heart for heart. This means my heart must live *absolute losing* with extreme care, so as to be completely open to the Holy Spirit who alone in me can worthily love the Heart of Jesus.

This means putting aside everything, always

losing everything, even the most beautiful and holy things; including all that I could legitimately love but which is not God.

FORGET YOURSELF

AT TIMES A sort of worry passes through your soul. In God's eyes what am I like? What dust, how much dust covers my soul? Even though it may seem to me that I have not committed sins, neither mortal nor deliberate venial sins, what sort of mess am I compared to absolute Perfection?

And to tell the truth we are unable to judge.

It seems to me that in this case the only thing to be done is not to analyse oneself at all. 'Forget yourself'[68] in order to look to God alone, to his will and to Jesus in our brothers. Be constantly 'outside ourselves'. Seek not our sanctity but the Saint. Besides this is where charity is and this is true sanctity.

And, as in other cases, here too remind ourselves that Mary Desolate has lost everything and therefore has also lost herself. Completely taken up by God, who fills this deep void, she is again the teacher in this work of 'forgetting' ourselves and of living life in God.

THAT CHILD!

JESUS, WHEN WE pray to you in our heart, when we adore you in the Blessed Sacrament on the altar, when we converse with you present in Heaven and express our thanks to you for life, when we pour out our repentance for our faults and when we invoke you for the graces we need, we always think of you, Lord, as an adult.

And then each year Christmas returns, a light which is always new, and like a renewed revelation you show yourself to us as a new-born child in a manger, and a wave of emotion fills us. We are no longer able to formulate words, nor dare we make demands on you, nor do we feel we can be a burden on such tiny powers although they are omnipotent.

Mystery silences us and the adoring silence of the soul combines with Mary's silence, who 'kept all these things, pondering them in her heart'.[69]

Christmas – that Child always appears to us

as one of the deepest mysteries of our faith, because he is the beginning of the revelation of God's love for us, which later will open out in all its divine, merciful and all-powerful majesty.

YOU SEE

YOU RARELY HAVE the opportunity to meet a saint. But when you do spot a saint you realize that sanctity can be seen in him.

Sanctity emanates from the recollection with which he prays, or celebrates the Mass or walks alone. Sanctity radiates from his face which is unmistakably supernatural, when he meets a neighbour for whom he expresses compassion, suffering and joy, sharing love according to his neighbour's spiritual state at the time.

THE VIRGINITY PLEASING to God does not consist so much or solely of physical virginity, but the spiritual attitude which is non-existence for oneself in order to always live completely for God.

It is the transparency of Mary, who never thought about herself but only thought about God, Christ and the Church, the mystical body of Christ.

The virginity which pleases God is therefore synonymous with love which burns everything like fire. Love which is participation in the life of God-love. God, who lives his divine virginity in his intimate life of perfect reciprocal giving.

The virgin is someone who advances without anything to lean on, alone with God.

Indeed, he or she finds support in not looking for support at all because God comes in to uphold them with help and strength when the soul trusts solely and fully in him.

If the phrase from Scripture *'Dii estis'* – 'you are gods'[70] can be suitably applied to any state of life, above all it applies to the virgin in the service of the Kingdom of God. The virgin is God through full participation in God's life, according to his or her capacity.

IN LOVE WITH GOD

SINCE GETTING TO know in depth the Heart of Jesus which lives and beats in Heaven for us, one has – through God's grace – new spiritual experiences.

When making a visit to church for example, when you are before Him and you say, *'I love you'*, the words truly contain the reality, not only the reality of the will, but of the affection, that *burning* affection which is human and divine.

Thanks to God, this really can be experienced.

May the Heart of Jesus, the burning furnace of charity, maintain our heart at the same degree of warmth as his heart, and may our heart be the treasure chest which contains this unique precious nectar: *love*.

Yes, love, the love of *someone who is enamoured of God by God*. This is exactly it.

So life here on earth is full, it no longer lacks anything.

'Heart for heart.' Yes, as long as the flame burns.

Then, even in desolation and in aridity, a desolate heart for the abandoned Heart of Jesus.

But always 'Heart for heart'.

Now we have a better understanding of, and repeat as something which is ours, 'Sacred Heart of Jesus make me love you more and more'.

NO LONGER WITH US?

WHEN A FRIEND or a relation of ours leaves for the next life, we say they are 'no longer with us', we think of them as being lost.

But it is not so. If we reason in this way where is our faith in the Communion of Saints?

No-one who has entered God is lost, because, if something is really of value in our brother, whose life has changed but not been taken away,[71] it is charity. Yes, because everything passes away. Even faith and hope pass with the stage of this world. Charity remains.[72]

Now the love which our brother showed us – true love because it is rooted in God – remains. And God is not so ungenerous with us as to take from us what he himself gave us in our brother.

Now, he gives us love in another way. That same brother (or brothers) continues to love us with a charity which is now unfaltering.

Rather, we should believe in this love of our brothers' and *ask* them for graces for us while we are still on our journey, and, at the same time, do our share for them by means of the work of mercy which tells us to *pray* for the dead.

No, our brothers are not lost. They are in the next life, as though they had left home to go to another place.

They live in the heavenly country, and through God in whom they are, we can continue to love one another as the Gospel teaches.

WE WILL NEVER understand enough the value of living the present moment.[73] Perhaps we should take heed of the fact that famous spiritual teachers advise the dying to live the present moment.

The fact is that if I live the present, God is with me in that moment, in both His will for me and in His actual grace. If I do not live the present, God is not with me and I am not with Him.

We often strive to find roads that will take us to Him, roads that will make us better and holy.

But why look for roads if the Way is Him,[74] and He stays there – the Eternal Present – waiting so that in each moment of the life we are given, He may enter into collaboration with us, in order to work with us and in us, and enable us to accomplish works worthy of the children of God?

If we need trials, if we feel the need for crushing blows, sufferings, mortifications and agonies in order to break up this boring quiet way of human life, so as to check the flood of the common current of the world and return to the pure heights of the divine, He will know how to reveal Himself in the present, under the painful and inevitable circumstances of life, under the perennial and unchangeable laws of the Church, which repeats with Christ in a thousand ways: 'Renounce yourself and take up your cross.'[75]

Basically life is simple. It is we who complicate it.

It would be enough to fix ourselves well into the present, with all its joys, its surprises, its efforts, its commitments to duties, and then everything would run on its own, as though carried by a powerful rocket towards the beatitude of eternity.

THE MAIN ROAD

THE MAIN ROAD to Jesus is his mother, our mother: therefore we should love her in many ways, but above all, by imitating her in her desolation.

The ascent is gentle with her. There are none of the great upheavals and inner tribulations which are unavoidable without her.

With Mary, as the saints tell us, our worst enemy, the devil, is put to flight.

With her the danger of spiritual pride which causes disasters is avoided, because where Mary is, there is humility.

She was present at our entry into the divine life at Baptism. She is present at every new phase of spiritual advancement, at every new stage, as teacher and mediatrix of those graces. She is present in every moment of our life, in order to help us to make our life a continual ascesis.

She will be there waiting for us, to open Heaven to us, and to take us to Jesus.

May I lose everything, but not Mary, Mary Desolate, in each moment of my life.

HOW CAN WE GIVE GLORY TO GOD?

'I GLORIFIED YOU on earth, having accomplished the work which you gave me to do.'[76]

It is marvellous.

So we too now know how to 'glorify God'. Our divine passion is to give glory to God. Now we understand that to live for the glory of God does not involve only cutting back our glory, when it emerges in pride or vain glory, but rather it consists in *carrying out* the work that God has entrusted to us, until he calls us.

Each of us has a plan which comes from God, and it must be carried out.

KNOWING HOW TO GIVE

THIS IS THE Gospel miracle which we must know how to carry out: to give the spiritual riches which we may have to our brothers, in the same way that Mary gave, giving even Jesus, and therefore, 'losing', but at the same time, not being wasteful, remaining empty, as we often can feel ourselves to be.

No, we must know how to give to our brothers through an act of charity. This new act of charity rather than emptying the soul, enriches it, adding to the richness the soul already has.

But how can this happen?

By giving, while at the same time remaining in communion with Jesus; communion with Jesus present in our soul, which means giving when it is the will of God to do so, and communion with our brothers, in whom we see and love Christ.

In this way we are in communion with Jesus within us and with Jesus outside us and there is no danger of giving 'holy things to dogs'.[77]

Yes, because this was the life of Mary.

This is the life of the most holy Trinity. While the Trinity was giving us the Word, who became flesh, the same second Person of the most holy Trinity was indissolubly united to the Father and to the Holy Spirit.

If we live in this way, and if we always act this way, through charity we will go from richness to richness, and we will be perfect as the Father is perfect.

Keeping spiritual riches for oneself, sterilizes the soul and blocks its path.

IN THE MAJESTIC setting of creation man stands next to man and the saying is true 'one man is as good as another'.

We are all human beings who were born, who live, and who will die.

Even if the spirit of the world leads us (and has often led us in history) to make a myth, a demi-god, of one of our fellow human beings, history itself has done justice to them, reducing them to dust like all the others. We are men and women who stand next to one another, nothing more, even though we have different responsibilities and tasks.

It is precisely this equality among men which *calls* for a superior reality; it is this people which calls for its leader, its king, its God.

Men, and women, have meaning if they meet in life with their Lord and Creator.

Then life is Life for man. Because in this meeting there is a fusion, an embrace, and the creature lives in his Lord and the Lord in his creature.

Life then is Life and through God it is *the* Life: 'I am . . . the Life'[78] Christ said, and Christ is God who has come to the earth.

This is true. And if it is true we must accept the consequences in order not to risk making life an exhausting chase for something which can never be reached.

We must offer our own will to God in every present moment of life, as an empty chalice, so that He may fill it with his will and with Himself – Life.

IN CHRIST THE TRUTH

IF SCRIPTURE TEACHES us to do little things well, [79] this is precisely the characteristic of the person who does with all his heart nothing but what God asks of him in the present.

If a person lives in the present, God lives in him and, if God is in him, charity is in him. Anybody who lives the present is patient, persevering, gentle, poor in everything, pure and merciful, because he has love in its highest and most genuine expression. He truly loves God with all his heart, all his soul, and all his strength. He is illuminated inwardly, and is guided by the Holy Spirit, so he does not judge, he does not think badly of others but loves his neighbour as himself.

He has the strength of evangelical 'madness' to 'offer the other cheek' and 'go two miles'. [80] He often has opportunities to give to Caesar what is Caesar's, [81] because in many moments he will have to live fully his life as a citizen . . . and so it goes on.

Basically, if someone who lives the present is in the Way and in the Life, they are also in Christ, the Truth. This completely satisfies the soul which always desires to possess everything, in every moment of its life.

THE EXAM

BY LIVING THE present moment perfectly, every act of ours, no matter how small, is clothed in solemnity, and when evening comes it remains in our memory like a happy reminder of a deed done perfectly. Anything which we realize has not been carried out perfectly, we place in God's mercy so that he can rectify it.

With this view of life the examination of our conscience in the evening is definitely made easier in every detail. This examination of conscience takes on enormous importance, just as the exam at the close of our earthly life is important.

From a certain viewpoint this examination of our conscience is even more important, because after the daily examination there is the possibility of correction and finding remedies, if God gives us this opportunity, whereas at the close of our life there is no further remedy.

If God allows us, we can go on living and take the exam again on the following evening with greater success, accepting and exploiting the suffering of all the imperfections of the days that are gone.

COMPLETING

JESUS SAID HE had completed the work that he had been given to do. He had to save us and found his Church, which was to continue his work.

However, on earth, He did not see the triumph of the Church or its initial expansion.

Yet he completed the work.

We often think in human terms about what God seems to want to achieve through us personally.

We set up targets to be reached while all the plans of history, of mankind and of individuals are in His hands.

We must 'resign ourselves', but with joy, to fulfilling what God wants of us, because nothing is more beautiful than what *God* has planned for us.

As for everything else, if we are left with other desires, they should already inspire us to feel solidarity with those who will have to develop the work which we have begun. In this way there are 'those who sow and others who reap'[82] and everyone shares in the joy.

THE MYSTERIES

LIFE IS COMPLEX, joys and consolations come, but more frequently we are adrift in the everyday grey atmosphere; physical and spiritual sufferings of every sort are not infrequent visitors.

We must be prepared for every possibility. We should never be caught unawares by any fact or occurrence.

The Christian life which mirrors itself in the life of Christ, if it is authentic, gives us this amazing possibility of facing joys and sufferings in the ideal way, without the joys speedily becoming sterile and void or the sufferings overwhelming us.

In this way the Christian life is perfectly grafted into man's life in a splendid fashion.

Man's life is achieved and fulfilled by the Christian life, which combines with man's deepest and most varied aspirations, raising them to a higher level. The Christian life answers all man's questions.

127

Even though today there is an excessive love of using fashionable language, and almost everything is dismissed as being old fashioned, let's be bold enough to say that what can assist the Christian to live this way is daily meditation on the mysteries of Christ's joy, suffering, and glory which are strung, like pearls, throughout the rosary.

Our Lady invites men and women to pray the rosary daily. Perhaps she does this so that each day they may find themselves ready for what Providence ordains for them, in bringing together for their good bitterness and sweetness, whatever the circumstances.

HOLD YOUR HEART

'WHERE YOUR TREASURE is there your heart will be.'[83] If our treasure is God, then that is where our heart will be.

Our living Mary Desolate in the present moment, which makes us lose everything so as to have only God and his will, helps us to fill our heart with the one Treasure which we should possess: God.

'Hold your heart and make it an upright lamp,' was the advice of St Catherine of Siena.

Yes, *hold* your heart, this 'blessed' heart which has so much to do in our Christian life.

Hold your heart fixed in God, our Treasure.

I CAN'T UNDERSTAND how it is possible not to fall in love with Jesus. I don't know why so many people only know him slightly.

When the world sings about love, a love in which a person is often idolized, it is because the world is looking for somebody who should be loved, and, unless this person is found, the heart is restless.

Jesus is not concerned with the law of Moses. He himself is the Law.

The passage in the Gospel about the woman taken in adultery is a divine masterpiece. How can we find words to express this, since no words in the world can comment on this incident.

He is teaching. The Scribes and Pharisees bring the woman to him unexpectedly. He can read the fear in her eyes. She has been caught through her weakness. He can read in the eyes of the Scribes and Pharisees their desire to catch him out, rather than a thirst for justice.

Everyone facing him is a sinner. How can he condemn just one of them? If Jesus had been an opportunist, if he had wanted to protect his reputation before the Scribes, it would have been easy and lawful – for example – to condemn the woman. But, as he will say on another occasion, he has come 'not to judge but to save'.[84]

Here we can see this clearly.

Then . . . he writes on the ground: twice. The silence! The insistence of the others breaks his divine silence. How noble he is as he gets up after writing the phrase which nobody expected! 'Let him who is without sin among you be the first to throw a stone.'[85] Then he has a conversation with the sinful woman and is not afraid of being 'contaminated'.

What loving delicacy, what irreproachable majesty, what deep humanity, gently bowing to support a weak human being who has fallen through weakness. . . . Then his words dismissing her, 'Go and do not sin again.'[86] And before that, 'Has no one condemned you?'[87]

THE SHEPHERD LEADER

'I AM THE good shepherd, I know my own sheep and my own know me.'[88]

Yes, there is a buried affinity, buried in us, between what you say and what we feel deep down. We know when it is Your voice and when it is not.

Thank you for comparing us to sheep that are good and docile: you are like a mother who recognizes her innocent baby in her rough son. You give us courage because you believe in our possible goodness; we thank you for this.

Life is a complete game of love: you believe in our love and we want to and should believe in the love coming from you.

You are there at the head, Jesus, leading those who know you and follow you, and also those who do not yet know you, but who will follow you.

Jesus: the only great leader of the world. We do not want to call anyone else leader.

He is unique: a shepherd leader who gives his life for his own people.

Have we thought about this?

It is something so great; it is too much for us who are blind and ungrateful and have our gaze always fixed only on the earth.

But you are there, Jesus, and you enable us to hear your voice, which wakes us up and we want to follow you.

'THY WILL BE done on earth as it is in heaven.'[89]

What a great thing you make us ask for, my God.

But who in the world does your will, and in particular who always does it? Of course, you are perfect and absolute and you ask for perfect and absolute things. Why else would you have come?

'Give us this day our daily bread.' This day. You really want us to live your way, Lord!

But who in the world, who lives 'this day', and only for 'this day', abandoning themselves to the future like free flying birds for whom you provide food and clothes?

Living for 'this day' simplifies but also terrorizes our human nature, which would like to abandon itself to a sure future. Yet there may not be a tomorrow . . . and you, Lord, want us to be vigilant. This is right, for you announce another Kingdom in the next life, to which we will be called on a day and at an hour which are unknown to us, and so you cannot contradict yourself. Therefore, give us the grace to live well each day established by you, for the rest of our life.

'And forgive us our debts.'

You do not say 'sins' you say 'debts'.

Yes, because sinning is not loving, and love is the one debt which we have in this life. [90]

SILENCE

WHEN ON RARE occasions I have the opportunity to recollect myself in a solitary place and I pray, I sometimes become aware of how strongly this silence speaks, a silence uninterrupted by telephones, radios, cars, or street sounds.

What happens is I realize that where there is noise, there is God's silence and where there is silence there is God's voice.

Not infrequently when I pick up a book to meditate, I find I have to put it down at once because inside me He wants us to talk. . . .

This gives me an understanding of the Anchorites, the Carthusians, the Trappists . . . how their life is filled with sound, how full it is and what great company they enjoy.

But I can only take this comfort from God as a means of continuing my work and for going back closer to mankind whom I must serve, so as to carry out the work which God has entrusted to me, giving this to him in exchange for his love and for the words which He prompts in silence, in the depths of my heart.

It is enough for me to feel myself called and to know I am loved.

This, at least, I hope for, solely on account of his mercy.

THE HOUR

GOOD FRIDAY: HERE we have the new value of suffering in our Christian life. I would say it is the call to the highest vocation among all the vocations we have each day and each hour of our life.

Jesus, 'the man of sorrows'.[91] This is the culmination of his vocation.

In our work and in our successes we are tempted at times to consider suffering people as marginal cases to be given treatment, to be visited, and, if possible, to be cured quickly so that they can become active again, almost as though activity were the centre of how we should be.

But no: those of us who suffer, who lie ill, who die and who offer everything for God, are the chosen ones.

They stand at the top of the hierarchy of love.

They do most and achieve most.

Therefore we should have no fear if suffering

awaits us. We must expect suffering to come because Jesus came for the hour of his suffering and we have come for the hour of our suffering.

•

I READ IN St Matthew: 'Blessed are those who mourn for they shall be comforted.'[92] These words impressed themselves on me.

If this is so, then the Gospel is really in complete opposition to this world which looks for every sort of comfort and well-being, not suffering.

Aren't all the beatitudes perhaps goals to be reached? Poverty, mercy towards others, meekness...

If this is so, the cross is not only a period of the Christian life which we must pass through so as to be sealed by the cross; the cross is the constant aspiration of the Christian who chooses God in life here on earth, a crucified God. The Christian seeks for this God and loves him and waits for him.

If later, as a result, we are comforted, this is a Gospel promise, not the result of our searching.

140

WE HAVE BEEN enjoying life recently in a way we have, perhaps, never done before. It is a pure joy, never before experienced, and it springs from the fact that we have made a discovery.

We can truly repeat a phrase which is the most sincere aspiration of the whole of mankind: we have found happiness.

You have to experience this happiness in order to know what it is.

This crystal clear joy cannot be anything but God. The God whom we find in each present moment, losing everything in the present so as to be only His will. I think it may be a state of the soul, perhaps a stage that has been reached. Hoping only in Him, we invoke the Lord and ask that we may never descend from this step.

No, because this happiness in us coincides with the glory of God, with the added glory our miserable soul (which yet is so loved by God) can offer him.

We have truly found the precious pearl for which it is worth selling everything, losing everything.

It is God. He alone who will remain for us, soon, when we pass into the next life, where Mary our Mother awaits us, happy to have been the *Way* for us, through her desolation.

IF YOU LIVE the present, but live it well, you achieve works which last, even, if you only speak to one person, even if you prepare a talk for one sort of public. Yes, the whole of humanity is in a person, and also in a particular group, just as the whole will of God is in one will of his. This totally satisfies you when you experience it, because you embrace infinity.

This means doing well what God wants in the present and doing it as God wants it to be done, according to his system, his dialectic. For example, it means preparing what you have to say with all the help of the Holy Spirit who is in you, and then exposing it to the fire of mutual love with your brothers, so that it may die, rot and be reborn from unity (and this demands knowing how to lose and humility), and finally submitting it to the judgement of authority so that it may be pruned. Then the talk remains and multiplies itself, and something that otherwise might have done a certain amount of good to one person and would then have been lost, does good to many and will continue to do good.

This activity in the present gives a sense of fullness, because it is the life of Jesus living in us.

And if Jesus lives in us, he achieves works which remain. If then, unfortunately, you have not done things well, or have half done them, 'lose them' in the Heart of Jesus with extreme confidence, with the knowledge of someone who knows that the Heart of Jesus desires only to love you in concrete ways and therefore to fill in emptiness, hiding your misdeeds from others and forgiving them, because if this is what a mother does, how much more can we expect from the Heart of Jesus? Here too is a source of complete fulfilment; everything is achieved.

THANK YOU

PASSION FRIDAY: FEAST day of the suffering *Desolata*, even though we know that a very special light comes from her suffering; that light which is celebrated in September, the feast day of the glorious *Desolata*.

Let us remind ourselves therefore that to be the followers of Mary here on earth we must choose the cross.

And on each occasion when the cross arrives let's say 'thank you, thank you' to Jesus and Mary.

But when joy arrives it's enough to say 'thank you' to them once.

More than once I have felt in my heart the impelling desire to have a second name, which would express a second dimension in my life, and that name is *'Thank you'*. I feel the need to make the days I have left a continual act of thanksgiving.

MARY DESOLATE! WE can have lost everything, we may not be attached to anything, but
something may still remain which we believe
we can possess, and ought to display, something we can be pleased about: God's gifts.

If Mary Desolate sacrificed God for God, we
must know how to lose God's gifts for God.
Therefore we should not stop to consider
them, not fill our soul with spiritual pride in
admiring them, but empty our soul so that it
may be filled with God's Spirit.

If we have gifts, they are talents to be used
under the sunshine of charity, which must
envelop everything. But then you must forget,
lose, in order to be solely love for the souls and
works of the Church and love thinks about the
beloved not about itself.

References

1. cf Jn. 19, 25
2. cf. Phil. 2, 6–8
3. Rom. 5, 8
4. 1 Cor. 13, 8–13
5. Deut. 6, 5–9
6. Mt. 21, 22
7. Rev. 3, 16
8. *San Pietro Giuliano Eymard, apostolo delli Eucaristia*, Q. Moraschini & M. Pedrinazzi, Rome 1962, p. 5
9. cf. Audience of 24 June 1923, op. cit., pp. 389–390
10. cf. Jn. 14, 23
11. cf. 1 Cor. 13, 1–3
12. Ibid
13. Ibid
14. cf. Rev. 14, 13
15. cf. Jn. 8, 32.36
16. cf. Rom. 7, 24
17. Mt. 7, 21
18. 1 Jn. 4, 16
19. In Io. Ep. tr. 6, 13
20. Mt. 26, 41
21. *Enseanamenti di Paolo Vi*, Vatican City 1967, V., pp. 912–913
22. Ibid. p. 913
23. *Bruder Klaus, S. Nicola de Flue*, A. Andrey, Vatican City 1945, p. 114
24. Mt. 21, 21
25. Rom. 15, 13
26. Ibid.
27. *Populorum Progressio*, Pope Paul VI, 1967
28. Jn. 19, 25

29. *Sermon on the Song of Songs*, 43, 4
30. cf. *I gradi dell umiltà, L'amore di Dio. La considersizione*, Bernardo di Chiaravalle, Città Nuova Editrice, Rome 1967, p. 21
31. *Life*, I, 1.1, c. 3, n. 15. Vol. XII, p. 244
32. *Insegnamenti di Paolo VI*, 1967
33. Rom. 5, 5
34. cf. Rom. 5, 3
35. Rom. 5, 5
36. *Una santa penitente del lontano Medioevo viva nella memoria dei suoi concittadini*, article in L'*Osservatore Romano*, 2 June 1967, p. 3
37. Jn. 4, 38
38. Mt. 16, 25
39. Jn. 4, 14
40. Mk 4, 25
41. Jn. 11, 35.33
42. Pope Paul Vi, in a short greeting to a group of priests belonging to the Focolare Movement during a General Audience on July 13th, 1956
43. cf. *Disciplina e perfezione della vita monastica*, San Lorenzo Giustiniani, Città Nuova Editrice, Rome 1967
44. 1 Jn. 4, 8
45. Jn. 10, 34
46. Jn. 17, 24–26
47. Jn. 17, 1
48. 1 Pt. 5, 4
49. cf. *Oeuvres complètes de Saint Louis-Marie Grignon de Montfort*, Paris 1966, pp. 184, 187
50. Jn. 1, 12–13
51. Rom. 5, 8
52. Mt. 11, 28
53. Jn. 3, 29–30
54. Jn. 3, 31
55. Jn. 4, 10
56. Ibid
57. Jn. 4, 26
58. Mt. 5, 8

59. *Il giornale dell'anima*, Giovanni XXIII, Rome 1964, cf. pp. 156, 157, 158, 223, 318, 321
60. Mt. 5, 14
61. Mt. 5, 13
62. Jn. 17, 21
63. Mt. 5, 23–24
64. 1 Cor. 12, 12
65. Jer. 17, 5
66. cf. Prov. 3, 13
67. Mt. 5, 4
68. cf. Phil. 3, 13
69. Lk. 2, 19
70. Jn. 10, 34; Ps. 82, 6
71. Preface of Mass for the Dead
72. cf. 1 Cor. 8, 13
73. cf. Mt. 6, 34
74. cf. Jn. 14, 6
75. cf. Mt. 16, 24
76. Jn. 17, 4
77. cf. Mt. 7, 6
78. Jn. 14, 6
79. cf. Mt. 25, 21; Eccles. 19, 1
80. cf. Mt. 5, 39–42
81. Mt. 22, 21
82. Jn. 4, 37
83. Mt. 6, 21
84. Jn. 12, 47
85. Jn. 8, 7
86. Jn. 8, 11
87. Jn. 8, 10
88. Jn. 10, 14
89. cf. Mt. 6, 9–13
90. cf. Rom. 13, 8
91. Is. 53, 3
92. Mt. 5, 4